Illustrated by Karen Bell

High-Frequency Words				
the	a	of	to	said

Editorial Offices: Glenview, Illinois • Parsippany, New Jersey • New York, New York
Sales Offices: Parsippany, New Jersey • Duluth, Georgia • Glenview, Illinois
Coppell, Texas • Ontario, California

A big bug sat on
the end of a log.

The pup ran to
get the bug.

The pup fell in the mud!

The pup got mud on the rug.

Mom said to get the pup in the tub!

A big bug sat on a
cup in the tub.

The pup got up to
get the bug.

The bug fell in the tub!

The bug and the pup
had fun in the tub.

Mom sent Diz to get
a mop.